POEMS FROM THE SOUL

The Path Men of Color Have Traveled
to Become Complete

F. Vincent Singletary

Order this book online at www.trafford.com
or email orders@trafford.com

Most Trafford titles are also available at major online book retailers.

Printed in the United States of America.

ISBN: 978-1-4269-6999-7 (sc)
ISBN: 978-1-4269-7000-9 (hc)
ISBN: 978-1-4269-7001-6 (e)

Library of Congress Control Number: 2011909667

Trafford rev. 06/16/2011

 www.trafford.com

North America & international
toll-free: 1 888 232 4444 (USA & Canada)
phone: 250 383 6864 ♦ fax: 812 355 4082

This book is dedicated to my Black and Hispanic brothers and friends, intrepid in their own way at some point in time have been an inspiration. A powerful source of strength and support for me in the spirit of brotherhood and friendship.

Al
Alex
Chester "Pome"
Dacklan
Donavan
Kenny
Sheldon
William

Each of my confidants are the type of man who rarely allowed life to get him down. That's one of the reasons why we remained such good comrades over the years, no matter what circumstances presents themselves.

Contents

The night is beautiful,
So the faces of my people.

The stars are beautiful,
So the eyes of my people.

Beautiful, also, is the sun.
Beautiful, also, are the souls of my
people.

Langston Hughes

Introduction

One spoken or to a written word, we start to form the manifest.
An inspirational message travel through the darken body
of water. Passenger on slave ships bond to a new land where
our people's future generations has begun.
We are men of color the leader symbol of our people.
Embarking on this journey for the truth and understanding
of ones self. Our Stories, Poems, Essay and Photographs,
Are all here as a welcoming tails we wise to share.
To our sisters, lovers, care takers, and mothers,
within our life as African-American and Hispanic men.
These words in which identify us are variance and similar.
Chooses of that visions are yours?
Experience our tales, which we need to be share from brother to
brothers.
One soul, with one hand. Here I stand holding a
Pen and Scroll.
I shed all those threads that bind and cover my body. The
same way when we entered upon this world.
Holding No Secrets or fears...

Poems

Brothers it's time...

Taken accountability,

Having a very definite ideas about what a man is and

How a man should carry themselves.

I'm addressing my words to you brothers

We are all we have!

The dust has settled after our Million-Man March.

It's a time of atonement and proclamation, now hold our ground.

WORDS, is a powerful thing.

Question, what that mean?

Our mothers, sisters and women words has uplift us

Brothers in a path towards the legacy

To become men, Kings.

Richard Wright (1908-60)

Author of the great Novel ~ Native Son

A continuance moment experience.

I have to write

I have to write, write that expression building inside.

Unleashing my words

Describing my expression craving to come live.

I need to write

Pen in hand, tears balling in my eyes, I will start writing.

My mother voice words guides me, our special conversations shared has given

Me strength to write.

"Thank you!" a silent cry.

Pen touching paper, ink on sheet,

I begin to write.

Our story start's now...

Father to Son in my hat
Chester Sr and Jr Vickers

You are me...

I am you ... Grow strong son
You look at me with innocent
In your eyes

"It says everything all right"

I pray for you everyday
Something inside of me changed
It happen to me when our eyes connected
The man I used to be, he's gone
I gave him up that day you came into my life
So I could be your foundation
Pure settle ground,
Building my son into a Strong Black Man

In or Out the Game

Street corner blue
Let up by the neon lights of the liquor store
Shadow of lost souls
The price of the admission is you
A shadowy figure leak overhead
      "That's Gabriel; you don't want to fuck with him.
He'll take your soul man."
Pimp
Hustlers
Gangster
Drug Dealers
Shot caller and Big Ballers
All the same

Creating a Foundation

To whom it may concern

My survival from the urban jungle, created of concrete and steel structures with a poor reflection for trees in the rain forest of standing skyscrapers. Upon my arrival home into a universe of peace, which is my own? The phone was ringing as I was entering my apartment. A doubtful hesitation to answer this call, but I reluctantly did answer. Which has? Alter the journey of my life since this day. The voice on the other side Sent cold chills through my body. It wasn't from the voice per-say but the person on the other side of the receiver. My mind went back into the moment when we last spoken together and the way it ended.

Why does my heart feel so sad?

Why does my soul feel so bad?

Here I was in a hazy while this voice was still talking to me. Their words didn't register until they said? Those words brought me back to be grounded, I was in complete another shark. I couldn't ready deal with this surprising news put upon me at the moment. So fleetly end the conversation, asking for their number where I may reach them back. Not before explaining how I just walked in the door and would Appreciate to continue our conversation after I settle in.

After hanging up the receiver that conversation brought remembrance of the past history came to light.

A loud yell, "This is not supposing to Happen!!!" I could heard those words but didn't realize when I said those words at the top of my lungs. Tears ran down my Mahogany face; out the corner of my eyes hit the reflection from the full-length door mirror. Displaying a man not familiar to me fully dressed, but looked like he just came in from the rain shower. When my body did started perspiring my head was still clouded standing their interns by my reflection soaked. Steadily my Body movement was overwhelmingly I motion towards the entrance which was dark lidding to my bedroom.

Time has lapped since the departure into my bedroom was I found myself currently emerge. Standing in the archway leading towards the lavishly design living room. My silhouette in bath with the glowing light from the moon over my shoulder. I still struggled enormously with a discrepancy of emotional feelings on how to handle a pending that conversation I received earlier from that person of my past.

Was our last time a gathering together that harsh some unpleasantly, mixed emotions shouldn't have been exchanged between old friends, brothers, homey bounded in being each other confidant.

Nevertheless I had other calls that need to be made. A mission was bequeathed me to acknowledge this letter...

In this letter one important journey Laron wanted me to complete as his last request to reunite the boys. His words awaken a similar wise. Once five young boys, grow up together into manhood where our friendship was one of brotherhood. Now he wants us to unite for the reading of a second letter which I would receive from him at a later date. The motion of my body searching for numbers I had not used for years. Was this like a joke in a bad comedy show. But the only thing I could phenomenon was that first day when we all met.

Summer periodically seems to be to diminutive, especially after lazy days and relaxation warm nights. Just hanging out on the block playing sports and riding our bikes. Reality hit while viewing a television commercial one late night stay up after my bedtime, a "back to school clothes commercial."

Now the thought has entered my mind, school is coming upon me.

Also the presser where I'll be starting a new school. It's like venturing into a foreign country all so new. High school at that! New challenges and strange people form different backgrounds that's a new adventure to be welcomed.

The last two weeks of summer vacation rotate into one night. The first day of school was present. I made my entrance as the door parted for admittance. Each step I made felt as all eyes where on my. I was moving slow motion everything around me alumna and fade like some special effect in the movies, "The Matrix." When I reached my seat in my assign homeroom I observe the faces of my classmate to maybe recognize a friend or friendly face. There was none at the moment. So I settle into my seat and place my backpack under the desk. While placing my backpack under my desk I heard a voice from a classmate calls my nickname, "STORM!"

I was knighted my nickname because people perceived me to be a quest individual never displaying expression or any emotions.

While listen to the most popular radio station, "WBLS-FM." WBLS, had a program featured called, "The Quiet Storm." Playing all the classic R&B soul music.

To my dearest Storm,

It has taken me a lengthy while finding the words to write you this letter. Since this letter is the first letter to you after years of seeing one another. I was scared you might be intimidated of the unknown message of my words.

I wise we where back in time to a place when we were closer. A moment in time where we were in that land of our own bound had no time. Back than your acknowledgement of all the experiences we shared was heartfelt. The pledge of friendship a freedom to communicate whatever was on our mind, or happening in our life. Those pledges made between Peter, Brain, Jeff, you and I. Being friends we shall be someone who has each other's back and be able to communicate and help one another in your times of need. Do you see where I'm coming from? My journey into my future I have to reflect on the past. Do you remember, "The Land before time?"

Now I'm using those principals dispense my services and skills in the community with disadvantaged children's like we were. That's a great feeling, but LA I have found it has so many secrets. Especially in the Music Industry, but that's a story for later when we talk.

UR boy,
Leron

What do those words mean?

Leron's, letter had me in a state as a captive audience with a continue search of answers. Transforming me back into a time of our youth where five young brothers and friends, forge their bonds. Each one of us had a common bond where our fathers weren't a major present growing up but that never define us, we had each other. The pledge of our friendship made between us pick up some of our needs in mentoring our journey into manhood.

Despite our family legacy recognizing the unencumbered father role model being present we pledge to make a different in our legacy. We maintain that attitude through out our twenties. Planning the future we dream of and hopefully achieve, finding comfort in the company of man.

"I am my brothers' keeper."

Brother to Brother

In the Company of Men

If only I had the chance to sit and talk to all you brothers and explain this journey we have to venture into Manhood.

What would my first words be?

"Stand tall my brothers, we have a long road to travel."

Brother to Brother

I once lost my way
Feeling of uncontrolled emotions
None of which can be shared,
Those emotional feelings longing to escape my body.
Through your eyes you vision me.
Voices within whisper quietly, "Stand Strong."
Now is the past, here is your present
Men of color all alone.
Being a color man, our images of who
We should Be Act and Protruded.
From:
The Wall Street brother
Blue collar brother
Brothers hanging on the corner
Brothers behind bars
My talent Brothers
A brother of all colors…
Find solicitude in me,
Brother to Brother

Am I My Brother's Keeper?

To be his protector keeps him out of harms way? A mentor, teacher and his life coach for guidance. But why are brothers killing other brothers'? Man of there same race even faster? This question has been asked or thought about more often then we can believe through time.

Scholars, teachers, barbers and back room street preachers, from the corner philosopher have all tried to come to some conclusions. With their numerous explanations, the most common factor is that black are angry and that forms violent. The facts that being oppressed bring about violence and rage they are an inevitable response to social oppression. But violent begets violent, brothers' who are killing each other are just trying to be dominating, controlling, and subordinating another person or group.

The violence from black on black has effective us all as a group of people economically and across the gender line. Where the distortion of entire communities reflects that violence figuratively and literally. That the survival as a race of people, we must stop committing acts of violence and brutality. The starting factor to refining our men of color, from the seeds of typical American maleness which has been planted into our psyche.

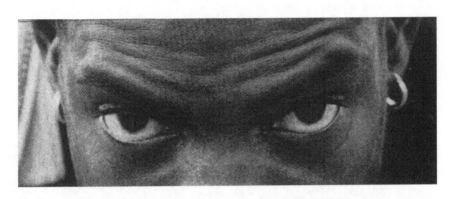

Can our young Black & Latino Men
Be Saved?

Chooses, Chooses!

A spit second decision without rational disillusion made on impulsive

Chooses.

Career assignment was stored upon me?

Reasons not sure about this assignment, feeding me your words like

A child bedtime fairy tale story.

While I seat in this interview wondering if this would be the biggest or

Mistake of my life?

Chooses...

Yen and Yang, balance of life, nature and creation.

The city grail a whispering cry when the wind blows sound.

I felt the vibe a beast ready to feed on its ground.

His meal is our souls; brother's Black and Hispanic.

Brothers joined from blood, love, friendship and spiritually united.

By Anonymous Author

A large Scroll Bandar greeted each attendee with the mission statement of the gather in bold black writing,

"The Coalition of Black & Hispanic Men," The Struggle may never end but changes come from within

I'm here at the first semi- annual meeting of the, The Coalition Of Black & Hispanic Men. A booming voice came through the speakers. Welcoming each man into the venue to take a step toward a new movement of ownership and accountability for our actions and recognize the future of our Generation which begins with us... As I entered Harlem gothic Cathedral, into a chamber of secrets, many men would wish death upon me. Where I chose to stop the valance against our people of the same race.

Each step I have taken, I silently pray Lord have mercy upon me. A sense of Death shadow over me. It's clear that I am here for a reason? Reasons to be reveal at a later time when the Earth and the Planets are aliened. Journey through the long hallway into a dimly light room, floor covered with misty flog smoke. Chairs were placed in a circular formation in three rows. Chairs are placed in a circle; because there's no beginning and no end where no one man will sit at the head of another man.

Today's Agenda: "Understanding the Power of Words." Placed on each chair is a copy of the Agenda topics we shall discuss within these walls. All our discussion here today are a message of feeling gratitude and appreciation especially to those females, women and pasterns in your life. But we have to mentor those young brothers to achieve theirs goals, aspirations and dreams successfully.

As I sat there in my chair glancing around noticing all the different brothers, to my surprise, I saw Brian sitting a couple of chairs down in the second row. In a way it should be no surprise to me because Brian has always been an activist and advocate for the empowerment of his race. Brian was mixed Black and Latino, "a Blactino," in the street term. He's stands six feet one inch tall, greens eyes, short curly hair and a golden brown skin. Brian prides himself on his appearance and structure, in how people see him as especially the young brothers on the streets. He and I would have many conversations regarding the appearance and style of dress we choose to wear and how people may receive the story it tells. Brian and I have very similar personalities and views on how we want to be received. I thought once the moment arrives I'll catch up with him to see how things have been with him since we parted ways to go to college.

The coordinator of the summit stands in the center of the circle chairs at the microphone. We are here gentlemen to understand the power of "Words." This discussion makes a bold statement. Words, are a series of letters to which sounds out in unit of language and a group of words create a sentence and manifest into a paragraph. A paragraph which convey a message that begins thought into a movement of reaction. Just think what bought us here today? The power of the words written on the invitation, got all of us to come here today. Words have many different relationship to the events that occur past, present and the future. Words can control the choices we make, how we feel, the way we judge our peers, and involute emotions. But we must make sure any and every message come across positive. Our message today is to be uplifting, inspirational and empowering. To improve on the state of our brothers who are in a transitioning period. We have to invoke a positive change not just for our generation but for the next generation of young men to follow in our footsteps. A salmon mood covered the room until one of the brothers who coordinated this venue stands up to address the room. He open his speech with a song from Kem's CD; Intimacy called, "Hold on." Following that song he resighted his speech, Back in the Day.

Back in the Day

I waited for some time to reach inside the minds of every legend that walked before me. These leaders, originators and innovators opened the door, for me to walk through.

It's like an endless ride feeling the lows and highs, wanting to give them a tribute. Celebrating them for laying it down and paving the ground. God I pray that their inspirational ways give us brothers the strength to carry forward their gifts.

I also wanna understand what made that generation of leaders become such ground breakers. These men have service their community and have had a successfully career in their various professions as well.

We start with:

Fredrick Douglass
W.E.B. Du Bois
Martin Luther King Jr.
Malcolm X
Huey P Newton

We have to look at some of our first:

U.S. Supreme Court Justice:	**Thurgood Marshall**
President of South Africa:	**Nelson Mandela**
President of the United States:	**Barack Obama**
Chairman and CEO of American Express Company:	**Kenneth I Chenault**
Chairman of Citibank:	**Richard D Parson**

When comes to the Music Industry we're talking about some legends such as follow:

Duke Ellington
Charlie Parker
Miles Davis

And one man would help change music today:

Russell Simmons

Today we make our move into an alternative part of history. History where we shaped the lives of our next generation of men with the actions we make today in the planning to become better man, brothers, fathers and leaders for our younger brothers.

So thank you gentlemen, for allowing me to stand here in great esteem in your present. The task before us is one which requires much previous thought and study for its proper performance to be achieved. In the current state of the Black and Hispanic men in this most diverse world that we have seen. Being habitat with technology and the vase new means of communication allowing them to move with light speed, far surpass our generation. Even with the progress of this country we still have opposition to face. From the struggles of the civil right movement where Martin Luther King and Malcolm X in the 20th Century worked towards equality. I refer back to a speech of Malcolm X called, "The Ballot or the Bullet," in 1964. Where he spoke of the economic of the Black Nationalism. Where it's was simply meant that we should control the economy of our own community.

1. Running and owning all the stores in our community.
2. Running the Banks

Brothers so let's re-educate, invest and motivate the younger brothers to take ownership.

Today we have the most wealthiest and educated young Black and Latino men in America to date in history. But for most, we must continue to in steal in our youths is the reality that they have the power to change things today. We have shown that with the first elected Black America president.

At the end of this speech we all clapped in agreement. On the second page of the Agenda was an outline for the Mentor program.

MENTORING:

Being an Mentor is extremely important part of a young adult life. The impact can be enormous and supportive building a relationship that last a life time.

GUIDANCE:

Walk through faith not by sight.

Roman 12:2

Create a Spiritual foundation, commitment it to a personal and collective wellbeing for growth.

SUPPORT:

Spending time to talk and listen to the Mentees. Help sharpen their thinking skills and develop an alternative ways of seeing the future path place in front of them.

DIRECTION:

Inspire to achieve their goals, developing a game plan for Economic, Social and Empowerment.

SUCCESS:

The Mentee are immediately introduce and exposed to a successful, caring adult. They will provide the Mentee with self confince and inspiration needed to succeed.

FRIENDSHIP:

The relationship received will help in a successful development Self-esteem and effective social skills. By teaching and being a good role model or friends where the Mentees learn the appropriate behavior in the adult world.

Street knows my know

Walk with me though the evolution where I came from.
Forgetting what bedtime story's told to us. My words come
from the soul.

"I don't want to be another static. A black man or a man
of color, branded a criminal." I wine and dine with the social
elite of society, who has committed crimes as easy as spitting on
wine. And they called me the criminal?

Though it all I'm still a Christen.

A bar code across the chest is not a badge of honor. I refuse
to be a static in the American blue and have the color of my
skin or the clothes on my back define me.

History of slavery chain where they change our name doesn't
stop the pride.

Today you're free to share the knowledge of the words from
brother's negativity the path of freedom to create a generation
better from their seeds.

BROTHERS BEHIND BARS

VOICES NOT HEARD FROM...

Having never experience being incarcerated, but conversing with a friend on a monthly base via a collect phone call from a State Penitentiary. Later, he sent me some Poem's expressing the thoughts of some of the brothers where feeling behind bars.

Behind these Walls

All Jails throughout the nation Black & Hispanic fill the whole population.
Some have family & friends waiting for them on the outside. Others believe their life has ended there behind bars.

I watch season change so fast, that when you think, you just left the past with trails & error much frustration. I do what's necessary to keep my patience.

Many times thing go wrong either you're woman is weak on she's strong. However you look at it you must do the bid the easy way out is to not live.

Throughout all my suffering I will not stall because I will receive my Freedom from behind these Walls.

By Sir R.D. Mack

Thoughts

In here you're mind is on key about everything, people, birds & the breeze. You're waiting to start a new life, whatever it is, it must be right.

I've seen many die and some are set free. Then I wonder where will I be?

When it's all over and I've moved on, remember to stay positive and don't do any wrong.

Wondering will God ever make a way for me to live long in happier days. Only one way to tell from lesson you learn to do Godly and get blessing you've earned.

One day I will be happy with what I got I know one day this madness will stop when it does I will work hard at being blessed. Because you can waste you're life in this Crazy Mess.

By Sir Reginald D. Mack

Whatever will I Do?

What will I do is what I say,
Be free, happy and doing the right things.
What will I do if I feel worry, should I break down and
Pray?
Pray to God and then be rejoice and merry.

What will I do during my heart breaking moments?
Ask God to heal you and continue to Pray until thirst'
What will me do- to keep from depression?
Pray to God to relieve me of my regression.

However, what will me do- 5 years or 10 maybe
How to stay positive and keep having the faith that will get me
through.
What will I do when I pray?
To ask for God his guidance to make a way.

Not only me but for people too
Oh, what will I do?
For people like me and you, oh yeah that's what will I do?

By Sir Reginald D. Mack

The Cage Bird Has a Voice

Blue sky, not unlike another without a cloud to be seen, a hot summer day this one stands far different from another to come. Being a youth, without a known cares in the world the hot summer days where full of fun, you know at that age. A wonderful time in our lives. Those were the days with the only thoughts and cares where all about than...

One day while hanging out on the block I seen Peter walking in a rapid speed towards a destination unknown to me.

I called out to Peter, "Yo, kid what's up?"

As he slow down for me to reach him answering, "Not a damn thing boy just chilling. I have to make a run for a brutha"

His tone and body language told a different store. It was a tone in a manner to push me always without saying it in words. I could tell it was a secret mission he was on.

Peter has always taken me under his wing like a brother. He became a big brother and mentor more than my own older brothers. Ever since I could remember being the youngest child in my family, my older brothers didn't want me handing around them. Now on this day there was a change that came from just a memory of yesterday, and days of my past.

Right now what only counted is Peter's words something I can't define.

The sound of quit, was louder than a thunder storm, fear was the reflects in his eyes. Here was that first day when Peter realized his freedom was gone. My eyes grow wide with the vision of the steel bars slamming close in front of me.

"Bam,"

rings like a nucleolus explosion during wartime. Here I am locked down, what I am going to do? Shadows of being a mentor to my younger brothers scatter behind me as the closing of the bars.

That first night was the longest night of life. Listening to the animals come to life in the darkest of the night.

Grand ma always said, "you made your bed and now you have to lay in it." I made my bed, now I have to lay in it. A cot behind bars.

A cot, a hot, and time is what I have on my hand. How would I deal with this predicament present?

Peter finds himself reflecting on the past, like all this is a dream. I have always been on the right track a type of goody too shoe. Especially compared out of all those brothers hanging on the street hustling. I had this clean cut looking appeal. The Catholic schoolboy, in his blue, green and grey uniform.

Know one never realize that the clothes I was wearing was not the traditional garments worn by my classmates. However, designers labels in the requite colors, a gift from benefactor. At that time, I never really knew what that meant. A new beginning the start of a new me and the end of the reflection that use to be of me. Now I have to reform and become, What society said I am...?

The jails are filled with black and P.R.

Family gives you Roots

Father's Pledge

1. I will work to be the best father I can be. Fathering is a daily mission and there are no substitutes for good fathers (I would study listen, observe and learn from my mistakes.)
2. I will openly display love and caring for my wife and children.
3. I will teach by example. I will try to introduce myself and my family to something new and developmental each week. (Helping with their homework and encourage them to be involved in extracurricular activities.)
4. I will read to or with my children as often as possible. I will provide opportunities for my children to develop creatively. (In the Arts, music, dance, drama, literature and visual arts.)
5. I will encourage and organize frequent family activities for the home and away home. I will try to make life a positive adventure and make my children aware of their extended family.
6. I will never be intoxicated or "high" in the presence of my children nor will I use language unbecoming for an intelligent and serious father.
7. I will be nonviolent in my relationships, (my role will be to stimulate and encourage rather than carry the "big stick.")
8. I will maintain a home that is culturally in tune with the best of our people history, struggles and future.
9. I will teach my children to be responsible, disciplined, fair and honest. Teaching them the value of hard work and fruitful production. I will

teach them the importance of family, community, politics and economics.

10. As a father, I will attempt to provide my family with an atmosphere of love and security to aid them in their development into sane, loving, productive, spiritual, hard working people.(To be activists and to think for themselves)

Haki R. Madhubuti

Teach you how to take flight

Rest your sleepy head upon my chest
List to the rhythm of my heart beat
It beat for you child, you are the key to my heart
Your hand travels across my face something you have often done since birth
Feeling that path that give you life and security where it's all right
I cherish every moment until you take flight
While I hold you, you are me
I'm what you see physically,
    Change together grow together we are united

Family gives you Roots

Storm the prodigal son recalls the impact of the African principles and history that we appreciated and could relate to in manifest our Destiny. Where it takes a village to raise a child.

Let's be clear;

We're seeing a change from generation to generation when more Black and Hispanic children are being raised out of wedlock instead of that two parent household. Some of these changes are educated choices made by the female or even by evens of nature like a death. But with that educated decision there's that? Trying to keep a man baby where after the breakup, she gets pregnant.

Up to this point I've been reminded of old times. Most of us were raised in a single parent or the father was not around as prominent role model. But that's not for every family around us just in our group. We have seen that there are families with that strong father present. We need to see more of them...

Focus on fundamental and values to be implement them in our young men. Distortion of the stereotypes; which brings me to this point;

The image of the Black man:

(Big, Dangerous and Scary)

- Masculinity

- Personal Challenge

From Slavery to Freedom

(Knowing where you came from direct the path to where we're headed)

- Plantation to the Penthouse

- Working under such horrible condition for a lower wage

- Working twice as hard as their White counter parts

Emphasized Education above all else guarantees;

- Brains, Success and good common sense along with a command of the English language.

Even with all of this some young man may still feel compelling to live the so-called, "thug life." Remember there are rules to survival in the streets.

Jeff stated knowledge is power- correct but there are so many intelligent people penniless and have no direction. But putting that knowledge into action and planning will equal the power of achievement. The challenge in creating a profound action plan must have steps of substance. The odds of achieving your goals increase tremendously when you see them written down in front of you and you can refer back to them.

Power of Belief manifest your destiny

Foot prints in the Sand

Where you an illusion in my mind?
I must have been image you standing beside me

Somebody knocking
Should I let them in?

Somebody knocking
When will that noise end?

My body falling
Down on bending knees crying out your name
My words flow like the wind brushing against my ear
Lord I came to you, with my soul weak confused
You gave me strength
You lead me on faith
Two sets of foot prints in the sand
Blind with clear eyes
Your strength gave me sight to see the serpent
Who wanted to catch me?
Do you hear me lord, give me your guidance,
I'm confuse
Two sets of foot prints in the sand
Then there was only one
Lord I didn't know you were carrying me then.

Birth of a new Renaissance man, know longer of the past 1920's -30's or 40's. I can remember a time not to long ago you where only five old looking up into my eyes the reflections seen was me. Nothing on this Earth I wouldn't do for you. When did time change everything?

Conflictions

Confusion

Uncertainties

You're becoming your own man.

I guess the rights of passage into manhood have come. Sands form the hourglass falling marking the end of time.

You stand in front of me now six feet tall; I still vision you as a little boy. Who once lied in my arms while you fall asleep? Where your hands would reach up and to touch my face, I guess than you knew you where in a safe place.

At bedtime I would read from, "Langston Hughes." So you can fall a sleep. As you gotten older our bond has changed one for independence. I nutrient your talents to succeed, but not to weaken you in becoming a reflection of my image.

Empower your soul
Empower your mind
Many black people in Business, Intellectual Activist and Inventors.

In the 1900's and through to day, blacks began to leave the South and migrate to the North, in hope of a better job and improvement of racial conditions. Often resigning in the larger metropolitan areas where there was heavy industrial development. I ran into Jeff one day, we had a conversation about a meeting he had with one of his mentor. One day I venture uptown into Harlem, on 125th Street. Seated in one local neighbor hood coffee shop which faced toward the corner of where Malcolm X once stand and made his speeches to his people. As I was sitting there I was transformed back into time where Civil Rights were in flight. He walked through the café doors into the coffee shop.

The sun bath over his silhouette outlining a man bigger than life to me. Skin of gold, hair of flaming red bricks like a fire house. His stature of a Greek god dressed in all black with a slim black tie.

He motion towards my direction where I stand to greet him.

Malcolm X, 1964
Photograph by Roy Schatt

A question of Freedom

Walk with me thought the evolution where I came from.
Forgetting what bedtime story's told to us. My words come
from the soul.
"I don't want to be another static. A black man or a man
of color, branded a criminal." I wine and dine with the
social elite of society, who has committed crimes as easy as
spitting on that wine. And they called me the criminal?
Through it all I'm still a Christen.
A bar code across the chest is not a badge of honor. I refuse
to be a static in America and have the color of my skin or
the clothes I wear on my back define me. History of slavery
chains where they changed our name doesn't stop the pride.
Today you're free to share the knowledge of the words from
brother's negativity the path of freedom to create a generation
better from their seeds.

Boys to Manhood

Boys to Manhood

Many steps walked in different paths from our first loves and the true learning of our bodies.

The journey of learning one self for whom we are is an on going process. We come from a family of a single parent home, a fatherless child or one with both parents presents. In the end we have to still become man. Being a man of color in America we have to endure the worst this country has to offer.

We have to become chameleons changing our faces even with one another's.

Your Words

Your words have given me the foundation to stand tall and strong
as your son, a man.
You never need to apologize for your words.
They have tough me so many things.
Teaching me that the person I've chosen, such
Be fearless with their love, not because she's a woman.
The givers of life and all that bull ship.
But because we are what all things start from...
A man don't know what he wants until he knows
What kind of woman he wants
Or fact that he really wants one?
For every boy, his search in life is to find his first love. A love in
which reflects that one of his mothers.
Indefinable!!!

Round table discussion

It's been a while since we've assembled together and enjoy each other company. Especially since we have grown up and went our separate ways. That ended our weekly hang out section at one another house. Those where the days back than, now since I received that letter from Leron and the plans to see my boys. Damn, time as cast a blanket over me. Especially not speaking to them wondering what changes has accord in their lives. This reunion will give us the chance to catch up on old times and all our new experiences we had up until now.

The mood is set with my stylish dark mahogany wood round table to play cards and a replete stocked bar of liquor in my newly remodel Brown Stone apartment in Brooklyn. I moved their right after finishing college and started my adult advantages in life. It's a chance of pace, being from Harlem. Brooklyn still offer that same vibe which I still find comfortable one of a family, arts, and a rich culture of history just rise from growing up, through the people, the architecture, stores and shops.

The door bell summons the arrival of my first guess. Peter walks through the door, he still looks the same just an older verge of his younger self. Peter was the oldest in our group a big brother sheltering us out harm's way. Peter altruistic action that day when I run into him making a run for some older dudes in the neighborhood. Later told the store why he acted the way he did? Rumor had it that Peter was arrested for possession of narcotics. When they stop and frisk him that was a basic accrue of the police for young Black and Hispanic men, they called it profiling. Now with that ordeal behind Peter. This gave him and I and chance to catch up before the other guys arrive. I can always remember how Peter displays this attitude and character which taught us to be tough and invulnerable.

"I see time has changed for you? Living the plush life now?" Peter commented as he walked into the apartment looking around the finely decorated dwelling.

"I'm doing ok for myself, with the help and gaudiness and education I learnt from school and my friends. You know how that goes? We all been there for each other, you should know how that better than anyone? With all those late night call we had." We both started laughing. I'll make you a drink well you settle in and we wait for the other fellows to get here.

You know we have never really talked about your incarceration. And how I would have been with you that day. But I'm glad you made it through that ordeal a better man today. Peter responds with, "While being in the joint? The states of the Black and Hispanic men are at a crisis." A few moments later the door rung again and it was Jeff and Brian.

Gentlemen time we discern our views of society has stored upon us euphemism with inadvertent of a crisis to Black and Hispanic men. Storm was saying to the fellows in the room. That brings him to the reason of this discussion; regale those experiences that we had until now this very moment. I couldn't only phenomenon what was going through our boy Leron mind. But in all incidents he must have been reaching out to us with this letter. We're living in strange and marvelous time, for our generation and future generation to come. The usage of technology has far surpassed when we were children. But we Peter couldn't help revive the trouble souls of our brothers out they're in the streets, since his days of being incarcerated. What I have learnt was some of the solution are mental? Jeff shook is head in agreement to that statement.

Brain conjecture with saying, although Black and Hispanic people make up over 15-20 percent of the general population they make up nearly a third percent of them full the prison population.

Yeah Storm added 25 percent of all our young Black and Hispanic men are in prison or jail even on probation or on parole.

Those static need to change!

Last Request

Ever since receiving that phone call from Sheryl, telling me Leron was in the hospital. She found my name listed in his emergency contract section of his Date Runner where he left in on the desk. Leron and I have always remained close friends like brothers especial after his mother pass and father walked out on them when he was four years old.

Sheryl and I once dated when we were youngster and she still lived in New York. However, since her performance in the school talents show case. She departed her life here in New York after finishing her Eleven year. In the High School of Performance Art when a talent scout offered her a role in a national film out in Los Angeles. How she develop an acquaint with my boy Leron? Their friendships flourish through me and later they became pasterns in sharing a passion for being talented singers. When Leron was heading out Los Angeles he got in touch with Sheryl who offer him a roof over his head will get started on his road towards success.

While Sheryl was trying to tell me that Leron was in the hospital I could hear something was wrong before she could even get the words out. That's when I decided to cut this conversation short and had to call her back. But before she agreed to that she made this statement sarcastically?

"It's a beast in the Entertainment Industry, there are definitely many secret..."

Surely after that respond there was a story not being told at lease at this time and I'm surely will get to the bottom of it! But before I could the second letter has arrived.

Hey my dude Storm,

As you well know by now that I'm in the hospital. The victim of a valiant beating, an act of Black on Black crime. Drifting in & out of consciousness, this has given me time to reflect on life and how much of a difference one person can have on another. Since we were boys we talked about a change is necessary. That's, why I don't know what to do about it and feel that as individual the efforts are not worth much. But as a group we are stronger, that's the reason for the reunion.

With my career goal of becoming a major recording artist, I can't help think back on a Rapper who influences me with his prays at the end of most of this CD's. DMX from the first time we all listen to his debut CD. DMX pray was a deep massage and always stay with me. The magical spiritual guided me to want us all to come together and form a solution and uplift the brothers and stop the violence against one another. Check out his words, "You let me touch so many people and it's all for the good I influence so many children I never thought I would and I couldn't take credit for the love they get,"

Yo, that's some deep shit, and I can feel what he's saying.
We're on a mission for God, let's start the work.

One, Leron

Recommended
Reading

Authors by Last Name

Anderson Ed.D, Cloud	Dirty Little Secrets
Baldwin, James	Collection of work
Cose, Ellis	The Envy of the World
Davis, Miles	Autobiography Miles Davis
Dickey, Eric James	
Douglass, Fredrick	
DuBois, W.E.B.	
Ellison, Ralph	Invisible Man
Garvey, Marcus	
George, Nelson	
Griffin, John Howard	Black like Me
Graves, Earl G	
Haley, Alex	Roots
Harper, Hill	Letters to a young Brother
Harris, E Lynn	Collection of Work
Hughes, Langston	Collection of Work
Huxley, Aldous	Brave new World
McCall, Nathan	Makes me wanna Holler
Mosley, Walter	Collection of Work
Parks, Gordon	A choice of weapons
Poitier, Sidney	This Life
Robinson, C Kelly	Between Brothers
Ross, Lawrence C	The Divine Nine
Smith, Dr. Ian	The Blackbird Papers
Strickland, William	The Future of Black Men
Washington, Booker T	Up from Slavery
Williams, Gregory Howard	Life on the Color Line

Wilson, William Julius   More than just Race
Wright, Richard   Black Boy, Native Son
X, Malcolm   The Man and His Time

MAGAZINES

Black Enterprise
Ebony
Essence
Vibe